NEW LUX KNITTING BOOK

1951 EDITION

76 designs for the whole family

New Aluminum or Plastic
HERO "JIFFIES"
Knitting Needles

now in
SIZES
11
13
15
also 9-10-10½

KnitKnacks
Much Ado About Knitting

Foreword by Kari Cornell

Voyageur Press

On page 1: A knitter knits and purls her way to knitopia. *Photograph used courtesy of the Library of Congress*

On the title pages: Knitting is addictive… pass it on!

Inset on the title pages: With Hero "Jiffies" Knitting Needles, knitting is twice as much fun.

On the CIP pages: Learn to Knit with 4-H.

On the contents pages: A 1950s-era knitter admires her well-stocked stash of Red Heart Yarns while her husband looks on in awe.

First published in 2007 by Voyageur Press, an imprint of MBI Publishing Company, Galtier Plaza, Suite 200, 380 Jackson Street, St. Paul, MN 55101-3885 USA

Copyright © 2007 by Voyageur Press, an imprint of MBI Publishing Company

MBI Publishing Company titles are also available at discounts in bulk quantity for industrial or sales-promotional use. For details write to Special Sales Manager at MBI Publishing Company, Galtier Plaza, Suite 200, 380 Jackson Street, St. Paul, MN 55101-3885 USA

ISBN-13: 978-0-7603-2847-7
ISBN-10: 0-7603-2847-1

Editor: Kari Cornell
Designer: Sara Holle

Printed in China

Contents

Foreword
KnitKnacks

By Kari Cornell

Kari Cornell is an avid knitter who's love of the craft sometimes gets in the way of family obligations. She's the editor of *For the Love of Knitting: A Celebration of the Knitter's Art* and *Knitting Yarns and Spinning Tales: A Knitter's Stash of Wit and Wisdom*, both published by Voyageur Press.

An Idyllic Evening
With the dog asleep on the couch, this knitter spends a perfect evening knitting in her favorite rocking chair.

Just One More Row
In this quirky Dutch postcard, the daughter checks to see when her mother might be pulled away from her latest knitting project.

I've been collecting pattern books, needles, and yarn—way too much yarn—since I began to knit five years ago, but it never occurred to me that I might have a problem until last month when I was on my first kid-free, pet-free vacation in more than two years. Rather than sleeping in on that first day of freedom, I awoke at my usual time, slipped on some comfy shoes and a sweater, and hurried down to the lake with my latest knitting project: a Fair Isle sweater for the baby boy I was expecting in a couple of months.

Without a cloud in the sky nor a ripple on the lake, I set up shop on the pier with a cup of coffee by my side. This was heaven. Over the next couple of hours while I waited for my husband, Brian, to wake up, I knit halfway through the band of color that brightened the tiny sweater's yoke.

As the sun edged up over the treetops to drench the pier in warmth and light, Brian appeared at the end of the dock.

I'm more than a little embarrassed to admit that my heart sank a bit. This was, after all, a vacation to celebrate our tenth wedding anniversary, and here I was, reluctant to put down my knitting needles and begin the first day of our trip together. And, looking back over the week and the enjoyable times we had, I still think of that first morning of knitting as the best part of the week.

Call me crazy, but I'm guessing that since you're reading this book—a book dedicated to those obsessed with knitting and yarn—you've got a few of these embarrassing I'd-rather-knit-than-spend-time-with-my-family moments under your belt, too. Well, take heart. The stories and knitanalia that follow should make you feel right at home.

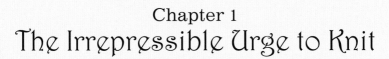

Chapter 1
The Irrepressible Urge to Knit

How to Tell When You've Crossed the Line from Recreational Knitter to Full-fledged Addict

by Laura Billings

Could knitting be so addictive that it's like a drug? Laura Billings, columnist at the *St. Paul Pioneer Press*, ponders the allure of knitting in the following essay, a variation of which was printed in the February 11, 2001, edition of the *St. Paul Pioneer Press*.

Excuse Me...
On this *Home Arts Magazine* cover from May 1935, the mother looks as if she is about to interrupt her daughter to see if she might knit a few rows herself.

Swing into a New Pair of Leg Warmers
Leg warmers and then some...all in one pattern offered by Hayfield Yarns.

I was trapped on a family ski weekend, three hundred miles from my stash, and itching for a fix. Then I saw my connection—a fresh-faced 19-year-old girl who called me quietly to her side and whispered that she was willing to share needles.

"I've got a circular size 10—awesome for your head, or if you're thinking of boiling it we could go all the way up to a 16," she said. "It really depends on what kind of experience you want."

I went for the smaller needle and without even sterilizing it first, cast on 72 stitches in a hot pink wool-mohair blend. Within minutes, I was totally zoned out, knitting and purling my way into an altered state of consciousness.

Many families don't know this yet, but next to Ecstasy, knitting may be the most popular addiction among our nation's youth. College girls—too young to remember the '70s, when everyone's mom made those awful rainbow acrylic crocheted vests—now think it's groovy to

32-38"

Hayfield

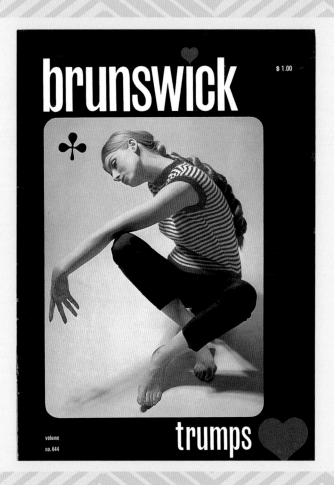

brunswick

$ 1.00

trumps

volume
no. 644

pull double-pointed bamboo needles from their book bags. Twenty-somethings—too naïve to know that legwarmers are not universally flattering—are flocking to their LYSs for patterns. And thirty-somethings—old enough to understand that knitting is really a life sport—are splurging for the classic cashmere that will keep.

These days, 53 million American women know how to knit or crochet, claims the Craft Yarn Council of America, a number up from 35 million just a decade before. The real surge comes from 25- to 34-year-olds whose new yarn fetish has spun off knitting nights at bars and baseball games, and even snowboarding boys who know how to cast on.

At first, this new hobby seems entirely healthy and worthy of that much-repeated moniker "the new yoga." There's an inner glow that comes from the tactile pleasure of using your hands for something more than mere button pushing. There's a natural high that comes from finishing your first hat and seeing the decreases come together in a way that is both purely mechanical and totally mind-blowing.

Knitting is the New Yoga

From the cover of this 1960s pattern book offered by Brunswick, it's obvious that knitting is indeed the new yoga.

Stock Up on Yarn
The very beginnings of a yarn stash...in a multitude of colors, and mothproof, too!

But too much of a good thing can be trouble. Type the words "knitting" and "addiction" into the internet, and you'll find dozens of weblogs written by knitters who are eager to confess to blowing the grocery money on fox fur novelty yarn, or who have called in sick so they could finish the poncho pattern they simply had to wear that weekend, or who post pictures of their sweater and scarf projects, measuring each day's progress against a ruler.

All seem in need of interventions, until you realize that organizing one would require you to put your own needles down. Aren't you the one who's *reading* about someone else's knitting? Who has the real problem here?

Then there's the word "stash," the term favored by drug addicts and knitters to describe materials waiting to be used for further recreation. Where you keep this stash may say something about where you stand on the addiction spectrum. If you keep yours where other people can see it, you're probably new to the hobby. If you've spent enough money on the stash that others would be concerned, then you

19

store it as carefully and secretively as you would a kilo of heroin. Mine is in a plastic mothproof box in crawl space of the attic, where the police—and my husband—would never think to look.

But drugs don't truly parallel yarn, since knitting doesn't cause anyone else pain. (Unless, of course, you've gotten into intarsia patterns of reindeer. Then everyone around you is suffering.) Some years ago I met a woman in a knitting class who spoke frankly about being a former alcoholic and the path to recovery she'd found through the Twelve Steps. She said that Step Four—making "a searching and fearless moral inventory of" oneself—was the hardest part. Following just behind it, many years later, was the pain of making a searching and fearless inventory of her unfinished Norwegian sweater projects. There were more than 30.

Her husband told her she was living in denial.

She told him she was just taking it one day at a time.

An Age-Old Problem
A Victorian knitter pauses to contemplate her knitting addiction.

The Knitter's Challenge

The knitter who lived in Eagle Bluff Lighthouse in Door County, Wisconsin, was actually able to set aside her knitting for a few moments...are you up for the challenge?

So is knitting actually an addiction? The addict says, "I can quit any time I want." The knitter says, "Just one more row." The line between them is as thin as lace-weight alpaca.

If you think you've crossed it, set the wool down for a while, just to prove you can.

And while you're waiting, word on the street is that needlepoint is a major trip.

Chapter 2
Knitting on the Road...and Beyond

A Few Ideas on Where to Knit Your Bit

One of knitting's finest attributes is that it's a portable craft. This is great news for the knitter who can't seem to put down the needles. Of course you'll just take that sweater along...you can knit in the car, at the dentist's office, at the grocery store...or at any of the places listed here.

Handknits on the Road
Knit a sweater for every family member using patterns from this 1950s-era Red Heart pattern book.

Take your act on the road.
In her book *Knitting Around*, Elizabeth Zimmermann writes about knitting on the back of her husband Arnold's motorcycle as they traveled to Madison, Wisconsin. A semitrailer truck kept pace with them for several miles, its driver glancing over now and again to watch Elizabeth work.

Daring acts of knitting.
A very brave knitter took out needles and yarn to knit a bit while riding on the back of a motorcycle as the driver circled the infamous Wall of Death.

Put your knitting on ice...literally.
In the cold, dark months of the Minnesota winter, knitters such as Amy Wilkerson Krause from Bear North Knitting yarn shop in Minneapolis take turns knitting on a massive scarf in an ice fishing shack on Medicine Lake. Other knitters welcome!

Knitting from the driver's seat.

Many knitters knit in the car while someone else is driving. Those under a tight deadline may try to knit behind the wheel while commuting to work. This isn't such a good idea.

Knitting on the job.
For those of us who are
chained to a computer
all day, knitting on the
job isn't an option. But
if your occupation is
carrying peat on your
back, knitting is a
welcome diversion.

31

Wolsey

No. 299
VIENNESE DESIGN
using 10 ounces of
"SEA PRIDE" 4-PLY
★
PRICE 2d

Knitting at the beach.

When you're sitting on a rocky beach under overcast skies, wearing the misshapen wool swimsuit your grandmother knit for you, who wouldn't want to pick up needles and carry on the legacy?

The perfect pattern for a hand-knit swim suit!

An old-fashioned knitting bee in the garden.
Let's see, you could be down on your hands and knees weeding, digging, planting, or finding other ways to get dirt under your finger nails . . . or you could sit among the flowers and knit with friends.

Strolling through the neighborhood.
Nothing like getting out for a walk and breath of fresh air, but wouldn't the experience be a whole lot better with wool and needles in hand?

34

Take me out to the ballpark.
Knitters gathered on a warm May
evening in St. Paul, Minnesota to watch
the St. Paul Saints battle the Sioux City
Explorers during the first annual Sip,
Stitch, and Pitch Night, sponsored by
Borealis Yarns and Ginko Coffee Shop.

Section
Gen Adm

Row
G/A

Seat
G/A

Price
$4.00

25532

Saints vs. Sioux City
Explorers

Sip, Stitch and Pitch Night
GINKGO Coffeehouse and Borealis Yarn

Friday, May 19, 2006 7:05 PM
Buy Tickets Online at saintsbaseball.com

Knitting in the parlor with a date.
Knitters have long known the craft to be alluring…but who knew the mundane act of winding skeins into balls could prompt such a romantic encounter?

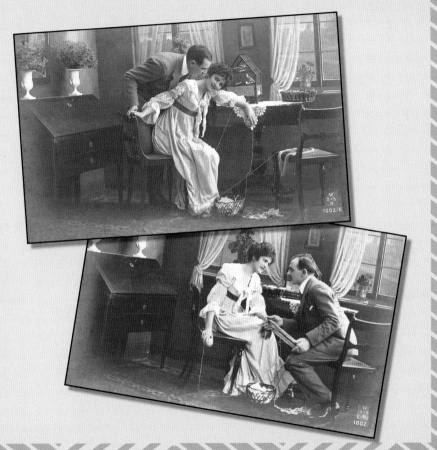

Chapter 3
The Agony and the Ecstasy
True Confessions of a Yarnileptic

by Clara Parkes

In the following essay, Clara Parkes relates the trials and tribulations of her own addiction to yarn, including her path to recovery. Parkes writes about yarn and knitting for her website Knitter's Review.

A Yarnileptic's Dream
Skeins of luscious yarns in a multitude of hues tempt shoppers at the Stitches Midwest knitting show, sponsored by *Knitter's Magazine*.

Yarnirvana
Knitting happiness is a many-colored thing.

To live with knitting is to achieve a state of bliss, an unshakable calm paired with a profound sense of creative fulfillment. The technical term for this is "yarnirvana," and it can take many years to achieve. To get there, most knitters first struggle with sustained periods of restlessness, twitchy fingers, and a need for covert yarn contact at all hours of the day.

The clinical term for this internal disturbance is "yarnilepsy," and it affects as many as one out of every three women in America. Early detection is difficult because it often skips a generation. And in its most infectious state, it can pass from friend to friend—and even stranger to stranger—from nothing more than an innocent, "What are you doing?"

Common symptoms of yarnilepsy include dizziness, sleeplessness, restlessness, a feeling of being overwhelmed, lack of concentration, and an inability to exercise any restraint in yarn-related retail environments. At its worst, yarnilepsy can cause total fiber-induced blackouts. Those who

Step up

YOUR KNITTING WITH GLORIOUS COLORS!

It's a pleasure to work with colors so gay and brilliant; so soft and subtle. It's a joy to make such a variety of lovely things—blouses, sweaters, stoles, dresses, afghans, mittens, socks and baby things—with superior, top-quality wools.

Always ask for DAWN WOOLS and CLOVER LEAF WOOLS at your favorite counter.

Sports Yarn
Baby Yarns
100% Angora Rabbit Hair Yarn
Knitting Worsted
Argyle Sock Packs
Baby Packs

DAWN WOOLS
CLOVER LEAF WOOLS
At your favorite needlework counter

American Thread Company

—MAIL THE COUPON—GET YOUR BOOKLETS!—

American Thread Co., Dept. SK-7
P. O. Box 217, Canal Street Station,   New York 13, N. Y.
☐ No. W-1 New Wool Book—35¢   ☐ No. 52 Afghans   ☐ No. 58 Kids' Sweaters
☐ No. 38 Basic Sweaters   ☐ No. 53 New Baby Book
Nos. 38, 52, 53, 58, 60—10¢ Each

Name (Please print)
Address   Zone
City
State   Enclosed $

experience this severe state often report an increased quantity of yarn and fiber around them when they regain consciousness— usually in shopping bags accompanied by receipts with staggering totals.

The journey from yarnilepsy to yarnirvana takes time and effort, and unfortunately many knitters give up along the way. If you think you may be contracting yarnilepsy, don't be afraid and don't give up. You *can* achieve yarnirvana, and its rewards are infinite.

After struggling with yarnilepsy for more than seventeen years and almost giving up completely, I passed to the other side. Let me share my story in the hopes that it'll help make your own journey easier.

As best I can tell, I contracted yarnilepsy from my grandmother during a brief Christmas visit when I was twelve years old. I caught a glimpse of her knitting basket by the fireplace. In it was a mound of butter-colored wool and an unfinished Aran sweater on the needles, bobbles and cables beckoning me. I felt a deep tingling

Yarnilepsy: It's in the Genes
A yarn addiction can begin with a seemingly innocent trip to Grandmother's house.

A Telltale Sign

If you arrange colorful skeins of yarn into bouquets and display them in fancy vases on your dining room table, it's a sure sign that you're a yarnileptic.

in my fingers, a quickening of the pulse, a magnetic pull between that basket and my body. My mouth opened and out came the words, "Will you teach me to knit?"

We piled into her 1964 Volkswagen Bug and headed to the local yarn shop, located in a cozy old New England farmhouse. We pulled open the squeaky front door and stomped our snowy boots on a sheep-shaped welcome mat. And then I remember catching my first whiff of that spicy, warm, lanolin-infused scent of pure wool.

Life became a dream. Everything around me started to speed and swirl. My pulse quickened. Blood pounded in my ears. My eyes and mouth were frozen open. The throttle on each of my senses was stuck in the full open position, with nothing to filter or slow the inward rush of experience.

Hands reached out to grab skein after skein. I buried my face into them and took deep breaths, as if in an opium-induced state of ecstasy. I wanted all of it—the colors, the textures, the smells. I wanted to possess that yarn, body and soul. My fingers

NEW! *NON SHRINK — NON STRETCH with NYLON*

Bouquet **Knitting Wools**

by Dominion Woollens

45

**Daphne
Crochet Wool**
Knitting is already a
pleasure, so knitting
with Daphne Crochet
Wool must be sheer
ecstasy.

yearned to wrap it swiftly and effortlessly around the needles, like I'd seen my grandmother do so many times. I longed to feel a sublime knitted fabric grow from my very own hands.

I have no memory of the next two weeks. It was as if I'd been abducted by aliens. When I finally came out of it, I was back at my parents' house in Arizona with only a pair of empty needles, a horribly misshapen scarf, and a pile of unfinished homework to mark my binge.

I knew no other knitters, and—with the exception of that sad little scarf—my house was devoid of yarn. I knew of no yarn stores, no books, no magazines, no knitting groups, no nothing. As winter turned into spring and summer, indoor temperatures rose to ninety degrees and my winter wool ecstasy all but evaporated. But it was just a matter of time. I later learned that once you've experienced one yarnileptic seizure, the chances of another one occurring are more than 99.9 percent. It doesn't matter if one year passes or ten years pass. The

Anything you Knit you'll Knit better with

Newlands

magnitude will be just as great if not greater than the last episode.

I grew up, time passed, the yarn returned, and the episodes grew more frequent. As the lure of the yarn got stronger, my ability to put it down weakened. I spent more and more time with my yarn—time that was earmarked for laundry, paying bills, buying groceries, bathing, feeding myself, sleeping. I was spinning out of control, and something needed to be done. So I tried self-medicating my condition.

I first limited my yarn contact to thirty minutes at a time, even setting a clock by my side so I couldn't cheat. But the very first time I tried this, I discovered three days later that the clock—and all the others in my house—had been continually reset as if no time had passed at all. (I still can't imagine why someone would've broken into my house and pulled such a prank.)

Frustrated and fearing I could never live a normal life, I decided to go cold turkey and eliminate all yarn from my environment. This, I discovered, is the worst thing a yarnileptic can do. It triggers severe YDD, or yarn deficit disorder. Even curtain pulls, shoelaces, dental floss, videocassette tapes, and jumper cables could get me started.

About this time I switched jobs and discovered a yarn store not five miles from my office. Lunches stretched from thirty minutes to an hour to two hours and longer. I tried putting just a little change in my parking meter to force shorter visits, but this only resulted in a pile of tickets and an eventual weekend at traffic school (a great place to catch up on your knitting, by the way).

I could handle the dirty laundry, bare kitchen cupboards, and questionable accounting practices. But it was growing clear that my career path—high-tech journalism—and my yarn path could not peacefully coexist. One had to go.

Avoiding the bigger question, I focused on climate. I was living in the San Francisco Bay Area by then, and the moderate temperatures made my wool-constant condition too uncomfortable. So I relocated to

Spinn, Spinn !
Röslein verblüht im Hag
Mich wohl niemand holen mag
Kam doch bald der Freiersmann
Führte mich zum Altar dann

Spinn, Spinn!
Once mastered, spinning
your own yarn under
cover of darkness can
lead to more yarn than
you've ever dreamed
of…and fibrolepsy.

Maine where, from a drafty coastal New
England farmhouse, I could continue my
career while expanding my yarn time in almost total anonymity.

Make Knitting Your Life

This beginning knitter has no idea what she's getting herself into.

But things only got worse. I started spinning my own yarn.

At home. Under cover of darkness. I figured that if I could control my supply, I'd no longer blank out in yarn stores. What I didn't realize is that fiber festivals—which I frequented for my raw materials—caused another equally contagious and severe disorder: fibrolepsy.

By then the yarnilepsy had spread from my hands to my brain, making concentration on anything other than yarn nearly impossible. Deadlines passed, e-mails went unanswered. My career was in peril, and something had to be done.

I decided to seek professional advice. My doctor, a young medical-school graduate who tried hard to conceal his smirk, quickly seized upon my use of the term "anxiety" and suggested I see a psychiatrist.

I went for one visit. Although the woman seemed competent, she kept referring to yarn as "string." Clearly we had no future.

I returned to the smirking MD, whose patience seemed to be wearing thin. "You

LIFE

HOW TO KNIT

NOVEMBER 24, 1941 **10** CENTS
YEARLY SUBSCRIPTION $4.50

**Minerva
Knitting Manual**
A United Nations' of
swatches adorn this
knitting book published
in 1951.

say your career is in peril?" he asked, tapping his pencil on my file. "Perhaps career counseling is in order." Off I went to the career counselor, a young woman with a tidy bob haircut, bright hazel eyes, a slim figure, boundless energy, and best of all, no smirk.

I launched into my story like a road-weary salesman giving his spiel, waiting for the shuffling of feet, nervous clearing of throat, and furtive jotting of the words "blatant sociopath" on my file.

But she listened intently, nodding in what seemed like genuine understanding and sympathy. When I finished, she paused before speaking. "Your career isn't in peril," she smiled slowly. "It just needs refocusing." Pulling out a notepad, she continued, "I'm going to map out a potential mode of treatment. It's pretty dramatic, but it may just work."

She scribbled for a moment, tore the sheet off her pad, folded it, and handed it to me. We shook hands, and she started for the door. I carefully unfolded the precious piece of paper. On it were the words, "You must

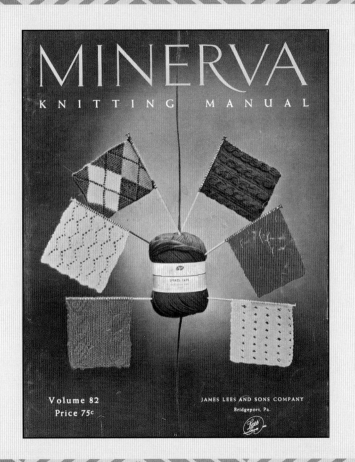

MINERVA
KNITTING MANUAL

Volume 82
Price 75¢

JAMES LEES AND SONS COMPANY
Bridgeport, Pa.

There is Money in Knitting
Here's an opportunity no yarnileptic should pass up...a chance to knit full-time!

give up your job and make knitting your life."

What?! I glanced at the figure walking away. She had seemed so smart, so sure of herself, so competent, and yet . . . quit my job?!

But something clicked in my mind. I began hatching a plan to bring heart and hands together. It involved taking my editorial experience with technology product reviews and applying it instead to yarn.

Nonknitters thought I was insane. And yet with each step I took, I could feel the yarnilepsy abate. My new publication, *Knitter's Review*, launched and grew. And gradually the frustration and twitchy fingers gave way to fulfillment and the justified presence of yarn all around me, all the time. The struggle with yarnilepsy gave way to a daily indulgence in fiber bliss.

I started meeting other people who, given the same advice, left behind successful careers to focus on knitting full-time.

Writers, yarn store owners, pattern designers, spinners, dyers, publishers, breeders, toolmakers, they all had one thing in common: they had battled yarnilepsy and achieved yarnirvana.

Yarnilepsy is a deeply personal state. For me, it's entering a pasture and hearing the bleating of happy sheep. For others, it's the magical moment they pull a skein from the indigo dyepot and its color shifts to an oxygen-provoked blue. Yet others experience it when they receive the first hand-knit incarnation of their designs from a test knitter, or when they see the glimmer of comprehension in a student's eye when she finally understands the knit stitch.

For me, it's the routine realization that my work no longer takes me away from yarn—it *is* yarn. It's the sight of heaping piles of colorful test swatches and even larger piles of yarn waiting for their turn on the needles. It's the sight of books to be read and tools to try. And always, it's the unspoken kinship and camaraderie I feel when meeting others on the same path.

Chapter 4
Will Work for Yarn

Signs that Yarn (and Acquiring More of It) Dominates Your Existence

Suspect you might be a yarnileptic? There's no need to panic just yet. First, read through the following list of symptoms. If you can answer "yes" to at least five, seek professional help immediately.

Knitting Lessons

If you're feeling guilty about spending too much of your time knitting, make it a family affair and teach your daughters or sons to knit.

You Starve in the Name of Yarn.

You begin to scrimp on groceries to feed your
need for more yarn.

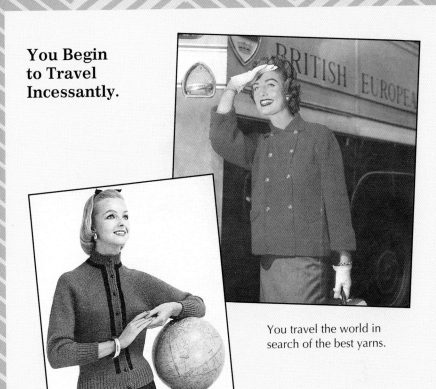

**You Begin
to Travel
Incessantly.**

You travel the world in
search of the best yarns.

61

You Suffer from Yarn Stash Amnesia.

You begin to discover skeins hidden away in obscure corners of the house, yarns you never remember buying. How on earth did that wad of shocking pink eyelash yarn end up in your sock drawer? You may have a problem.

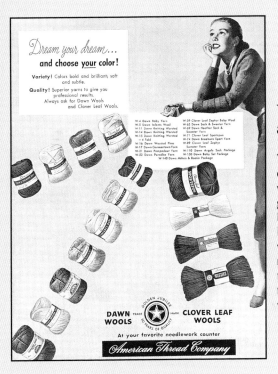

You Daydream about Yarn

You find yourself daydreaming about when you'll be able to get your next yarn fix. Perhaps you can take a long lunch and run to the yarn shop . . .a mere five minutes in a room full of fiber would do wonders for your peace of mind, you reason.

When you close your eyes to go to sleep you see yarn, in all colors of the rainbow. When you do finally fall asleep you dream bizarre dreams of chickens knitting claw-shaped gloves.

Visions of Yarn and Knitting Disturb Your Sleep.

You Stock up on Unusual Knitting Supplies.

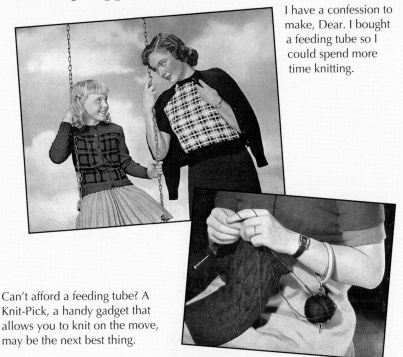

I have a confession to make, Dear. I bought a feeding tube so I could spend more time knitting.

Can't afford a feeding tube? A Knit-Pick, a handy gadget that allows you to knit on the move, may be the next best thing.

You Consider Tending Sheep.

Even though you live in a small turn-of-the-century home on a city lot, you fence in your yard and entertain the idea of someday buying a few sheep to fuel your addiction.

You Decide the Cure for What Ails you may be to Buy More Yarn.

You join a knitting club at a local yarn shop so you have easier access to a steady supply. *Photo used courtesy of the Minnesota Historical Society*

You Look for Openings at the Local Knitting Mill.

You dream of days gone
by, when a job at a
knitting mill was much
easier to obtain.

Dressed in their latest handknit items, two knitters scour the want ads for that dream job.

Two-dresses-in-one are yours with this reversible outfit, thanks to a unique new stitch that's just as attractive on one side as the other. It's a version of cable-stitch that gives the effect of an occasional soft knot, breaking the long up-and-down lines of the blouse. The slimming lines of the skirt, however, are left unbroken. The pullover and skirt are separate. But if you'd prefer a one-piece dress, leave off the ribbing and join skirt and blouse with crocheted beadings and elastic.

MINERVA

HAND-KNITS IN NYLON FOR THE FAMILY

PRICE 35¢
VOLUME 77

Chapter 5
Ridiculous Knits

Knitting for the Man in Your Life

by Sigrid Arnott

If your knitting time begins to infringe noticeably on your family time, ease the guilt by knitting gifts for family members. In the following essay, Sigrid Arnott offers a few tips on knitting gifts for the one you're most likely going to have to appease: your husband.

Handknits in Nylon For the Family
In 1948, Minerva offered patterns for matching cabled vests for every member of the family. Now, how could a knitter possibly go wrong?

Smart Knitwear for Men

Wartime knitting books offered plenty of streamlined sweaters and accessories for men...all knit on size 1 and 2 needles.

BOOK 2

SMART KNITWEAR FOR MEN

17 Exclusive Service Garments approved by the Canadian Red Cross and the Imperial Order Daughters of the Empire.

Civilian Sweaters and Accessories.

The desire to create something for those we love seems to be ingrained into every knitter's psyche. It feels so good to find just the shade of orange your best friend loves and make a long scarf with wacky fringe for her to wrap around her neck. Felted mittens in bright colors are just the thing to warm the hands of cold kids. And what could be more satisfying than seeing a baby modeling a quirky hat you designed? Knitting these one-of-a-kind scarves, mitts, and baby things doesn't require a huge investment of money or time, so we can give them freely and generously, not worrying that they will someday be lost, destroyed, outgrown.

Men, however, present a knitting challenge. The urge to stitch for them is often over-ruled by our well-founded suspicion that they won't want to wear what we want to make.

"What makes her think she is such an expert on guys?" you may be wondering. Well, let me tell you, I grew up with two older brothers who taught me everything they thought I needed know. Because of a demographic fluke, one year I was the only girl in my school. My husband comes from a family of boys, all of whom have lived under my roof—sometimes all at the same time. And I now have two sons. As a child, I couldn't knit, but I made rope with Dad. I never learned how to apply eyeliner, but I can throw a mean punch. So, stick with me; I know some things.

The biggest problem with guys is that they are boring.

For one thing, men only wear colors when they are Team Colors. But even then they can't just wear, say, any old shade of green and yellow from your stash. Guys want Packer Green with Packer Yellow. One thing yarn companies haven't realized is that there's a market for handpainted yarns in team-sponsored colors, if they would come with little tags for the NBA, NFL, NHL,

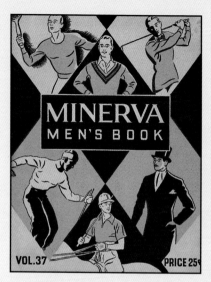

Minerva Men's Book
For only 25 cents, a knitter in the 1930s looking for the perfect sweater for the man in their life had access to this treasure-trove of patterns offered by Minerva.

NASCAR, or N-whatever. The male of our species is infatuated with authorized sportswear, and that little tag makes them feel secure wearing colors.

If a man isn't into sports, he will just wear black, gray, and navy—sometimes all at the same time. I hate knitting anything solid black, gray, or navy. I can't even force myself to buy yarns in those colors, and believe me, when it comes to yarn I usually have to hold myself back. It can be hard to start a project if you can't bring yourself to purchase the yarn.

The next problem with knitting for guys is that men are indifferent to wooly accessories and refuse to wear mittens. The one exception to this rule is the boring black watch cap. All men, almost without exception, love black watch caps knit in fine-gauge, ribbed acrylic. Sometimes they will accept a hat in another color, like dark green, if it has a tag on the outside affiliated with something manly, like a rock band or a brand of work clothing. We have about twenty of these in our house, and the guys still fight over them. Men just don't know that in the time it would take you to make a little black watch cap in a fine-gauge yarn, on size 1 needles in one-by-one rib, you could make yourself a fantastic sweater. Then, should they put it on and mention that it's a little itchy around their forehead, they would be surprised to have five US size 1 double-point knitting needles fly toward their black watch–capped head.

Which brings up problem number three. Although men are solid and strong and often covered with prickly hairs, they are also delicate. Guys cannot abide anything knit with wools containing any coarse fibers or tickly hairs. I am convinced that the models for the Lopi books have been drugged with sedatives, or else their faces have been digitally altered to erase the aggrieved look of the hair-shirted hermit. It's a knitter's paradox that men want rugged-looking

The Dreaded Watch Cap

Called the "Sleeping Cap" in this 1917 Columbia Yarns pattern book, here's that dreaded pattern, spelled out in black and white.

MATERIAL

Columbia Worsted Knitting Yarn

1 hank
4 Celluloid or Bone double pointed Knitting Needles No. 4

INSTRUCTIONS

Cast on 96 stitches, 32 on each of the 3 needles, now knit 2, purl 2, for 35 rows, then knit 6, purl 2 for 22 rows, now decrease 1 stitch at each end of each needle every row until 4 stitches remain on each needle, break the yarn off leaving about 1 yard, thread this into a large needle, draw through all stitches, draw stitches together and sew firmly in place.

King-Size Man

This ad for King-Size clothing that appeared in a 1970s *Woman's Day Knitting Book* captures the sentiment of every knitter who wants to knit a sweater for their beloved.

Have you any idea what it means
to fall in love with a King-Size man?
(confessions of a big man's wife)

It means kingsize beds. It means aisle seats at the movies. It means running when he's walking. It means holding my breath while he tries on his new jacket.

For the clothes he wore never seemed to fit him correctly. I'd almost cry to see my handsome man in skimpy shirts or slacks, or a jacket that looked two sizes too small. Nothing he wore was designed or proportioned right for a man his size.

I thought that by shopping for him myself I could change all that. In our town there are many good men's stores. I shopped in each of them. But any shirt or slacks or jacket I chose, it was always the same answer, "Sorry, M'am, we don't have it in *that* size!"

Then one day a friend showed me the new KING-SIZE Catalog. It was a revelation! I could see *these* people were BIG MEN Specialists. They *understood*. For here was 144 pages crammed with smart, stylish clothing and shoes...sweaters, slacks and jackets... all specially designed for TALL and BIG men! Necks to 22"...sleeves to 38"...inseams up to 42"...sizes to XXXL! And the finest brands—McGregor, Arrow, Manhattan, Jantzen, Weldon. 200 shoe styles in sizes from 10 to 16, widths AAA to EEE...including DuPont Corfam, Hush Puppies, Bates Floaters and others.

Best of all, this beautiful full-color KING-SIZE Catalog doesn't cost a penny. And every item carries the famous KING-SIZE Money-Back Guarantee. "You must be completely satisfied both BEFORE and AFTER wearing, or you get an immediate refund or exchange." Could anything be fairer?

If your husband (son, brother, boyfriend) has the same kind of King-Size problem, you can solve it the same way I did. Just sit down and write for the FREE KING-SIZE Catalog. When it comes, you and your TALL and BIG man will discover how much FUN buying the right clothes for your KING-SIZE man can be

The KING-SIZE Co., 802 King-Size Bldg., Brockton, Mass.

The KING-SIZE CO., 802 King-Size Bldg., Brockton, Mass.

Gentlemen:

I'm tired of dashing from store to store unable to find clothes for my big man. Please rush me your FREE Full-Color, 144-page Catalog of Apparel and Footwear.

Name _____

Address _____

City _____

State _____ Zip _____

7

wooly clothes, but have cashmere-craving nerve endings. Now most of us would love to knit a something out of cashmere, but here we come to another guy problem.

What men really want are sweaters, *but* (problem number four) they are big. Even the smallest guy has much greater square footage to cover than the largest baby. Most guys have frames that effortlessly swallow up several thousands of yards of yarn, and thus what feels like thousands of dollars in yarn and thousands of hours of knitting time.

Also, guys don't like fitted sweaters; they like ease. Maybe you could knit a large, easy-fitting sweater for a guy with just a *few* thousand yards of yarn, but then you would have to use a bulky yarn. Unfortunately, most bulky yarn is itchy or available only in trendy, female-friendly, space-dyed colors. Cotton yarn can't be bulky because it doesn't have the loft. A bulky cotton sweater for a big guy would probably weigh 35 pounds and stretch down to his knees. Only wool from coarse-haired animals seems to have

Hand Knits by *Beehive*

ARGYLE PATTERNS
for
MEN and WOMEN

DAVIS KNIT SHOP

25¢
Book No. 140

the properties that allow for spinning a lofty, lightweight yarn.

There are books with sweaters to knit for men. The books bear titles like *Mainly Manly Knitting* or *Simple Sweaters for Simple Guys*. One of the current books has the subtitle, "Sweaters to Knit that He WILL Wear." (I'm not making this up, not even the all caps bit.) I was wondering if I should buy the book to get some hints on force-dressing males, but it turns out the idea is to look at what the man you wish to knit for likes to wear and let that be your knitting guide. Which brings us back to the black watch cap.

Perhaps I have given you the idea that I won't knit for men. It's true, the last interesting thing I knitted my husband, an Andean-style hat inspired by his favorite Italian coffee cup (maybe the mixed inspirations were the problem . . .), has stayed in the attic through the last few winters with the mittens. (Not only was it a little itchy, he pointed out that the dye in the red stripes bled when he played hockey and made

Argyle Patterns
A fetching pattern for an argyle sweater made this cover model a satisfied customer in the 1950s, but it's doubtful the sweater would bring the same results today.

Red Heart Sweaters

Knit him something he loves and you'll reap the reward.

him look eternally wounded. Curses to you black acrylic watch caps!) I have made him socks, and he does wear them, but sometimes a girl wants to branch out a little.

But I haven't given up; I am thinking along new lines. I want to use fun materials and try new techniques like lace, bobbles, and colorwork. Yet I'm not going to waste my time making garments that won't be worn.

Books and articles on knitting for men emphasize that the knitter should research what her man already likes to wear before embarking on a project. Take this idea in a different direction and comb through your man's magazine and catalog collection to find the stuff he covets. Interestingly, none of it is clothing.

Have you noticed that, except when feeling itchy, many guys have only a sketchy sense of their own body—but an intimate awareness of the state of their *stuff*? To show them you care, knit something for their gear.

Does your man have a big vehicle with a trailer ball? Mention some time that it

SWEATERS
For the Family

looks a little exposed just sitting out there in the elements. Ask him if he thinks UV rays might damage the chrome. During the time he starts thinking it may be time to go look for a Hitch Ball Cozy, you can knit one up. After all, it need only be about the size of a baby bootie and you only have to make one. Use fuzzy yarn.

For some guys, cars are less about towing and more about style. The sky's the limit when it comes to accessorizing a car, but here are some suggestions: knit an I-Cord Antenna Cover! The more conservative type might want a novelty yarn with metallic glints to match the car trim, sporty types might want team colors with a pompon. Lucky Dice are always in. Just make 12 little squares and sew and stuff into two cubes. Why not experiment with bobbles or intarsia for the dots? And by using an herbal stuffing (calming lavender perhaps?) you can justify getting rid of the nasty car deodorizer, too.

I love felting, and the resulting hefty matte fabric seems as if it should be guy-friendly. But most men just don't want the typical felted bags, bowls, or baseball caps I keep seeing patterns for. I've been thinking about making a Remote Holster for his inner cowboy. Modeled after the six-shooter holster, the modern-day man could always have the channel changer or disc switcher at the ready for a quick draw. Make a belt about three times too big with pouches for various electronic controllers, then shrink it to size and attach d-rings to one belt end for size adjustment. As this will be worn over jeans, you could even use some of those coarser yarns that come in great colors.

"What about the guy in a band?" you ask. Just as you need a little bag for your stitch markers and point protectors, he might like a Pick/Plectrum Pouch. As long as the design incorporates a secure closure and duct tape, it should be acceptable.

Speaking of duct tape, when knitting for guys, you might want to bypass the local yarn shoppe and head over to the local hardware store. Like the women at the

knitting shop who have given you so many helpful hints over the years, the hardware store guys are full of practical advice, and they can turn you on to some new fibers, some of which come in really exciting colorways. As an added bonus, none of them (the fibers, not the guys) require tiresome washing, let alone expensive dry cleaning. And instead of buttons or ribbon, you can find tough trimmings like grommets, ball chain, and mini-padlocks.

Twine, another great hardware store find, comes in neutrals and has amazing stitch definition and body. Cast on about 20 stitches, in a 1-ply, 8-pound load limit sisal twine, experiment with a new stitch pattern for about eight inches, and bind off. Sew up two sides and you have an Exfoliating Bath Mitt for the male with an itchy back. Even if it's in a lace pattern, the twine will make it cool and guy-approved. The yardage for twine can be fantastic with a few thousand feet of twine only setting you back ten bucks—that's enough twine to scrub several backs. Jute is softer than sisal and comes

Spinnerin Style, circa 1960

What men fail to realize is that women find handknits (and ski boots with tight ski pants) irresistible.

**Newlands
Cable Pullover**
Handknits and power
tools go hand-in-hand.

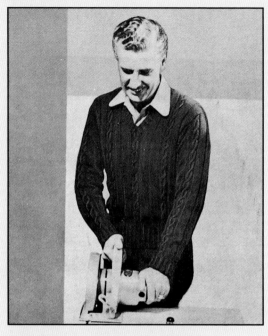

in natural or dyed green, but it also costs
more for a lower load limit. Jute's ideal for
the man with sensitive skin.

Mason's twine comes in basic white
as well as bright yellow and neon pink or

green. Because it is made from pure nylon, this stuff is seriously slippery, but it will never stretch out of shape or pill. Make your guy something that will take advantage of these properties, while storing something close to his heart. Have you noticed that guys worldwide like baseball caps—but haven't worked out good storage solutions for their collections? My dad shoved all his gimme hats from seed companies and fuel oil co-ops into a musty cupboard. My husband's retro baseball hats (all with tags verifying their authenticity) sit on his dresser smashed under piles of laundry.

I think the time is right for a Baseball Hat Hammock made with mason's twine in a fun stripe pattern, using huge needles. Really big needles can be hard to find, but the guys at the hardware store can help you find dowels and drawer knobs to make your own. The slippery nylon will fray easily when cut; stop fraying by melting the ends with a match. Attach metal rings to the corners and suspend the hammock from the ceiling over his dresser.

Some guys come with lots of cables and cords. They like to wind them up just so, but they still coil out of control. Maybe you have been thinking about lace and the feeling of satisfaction that comes from making orderly designs with yarn overs and decreases. Well, forget the shawl; get big needles and knit an Electrical Cable Snood from construction twine. (In case you forgot, snoods are those lacey bags one ties around one's unruly hair bun.) Just follow the pattern for a circular shawl or doily and make a series of eyelets around the edge before binding off. Weave a nylon-core, braided-cover rope through the eyelets, then knot the ends using a double-overhand knot. The cables can be placed on the snood and the edges gathered and tied up for cord control.

Shrugs are in right now; knitting magazines keep printing patterns for cute lacey numbers. I also keep seeing gorgeous shawls covered with weighty beading. What's a girl to do if she wants to knit one of these up, but needs to focus on her darling's upcoming birthday? Try to combine the two ideas and make a Beaded Car Seat Shrug for sticky-seat weather. Multi-ply seine string is strong (that high load limit!) and can easily be prestrung with large wooden beads. A broad-backed, thick-armed shrug incorporating a beaded lace motif from a shawl pattern, should be placed on the seat with the front-opening face down.

During the scarf-knitting craze, nearly every knitter became acquainted with creative multistranding. Apply that concept to manly materials and you can knit a special Good Grip Beer Can Holder with a melange of twine and rubber weather stripping. Stainless wire with rope combines for an Anti-Static Floor Mat.

In a perfect world, we would all be moved to create something unique for the ones we love, and the recipient would always love it. In the meantime, I will lay on the couch and knit my honey a ridiculous knit: I'm thinking of finger knitting a Bungee Cord Cargo Carrier—in racing red, of course.

Chapter 6
Knit Talk

A Knitter's Translate-o-Matic

By Sigrid Arnott

Sometimes we want to share our deepest feelings with those we love. What's one to do when those feelings revolve around knitting, and the one close to us is a guy? To avoid inducing that glazed-over look in him, use this guide to translate knit talk into a topic you can enjoy discussing together.

Knit Talk

In their 1936 living room, a husband and wife connect using the Knitter's Translate-o-Matic.

Knitting Language	Guy Talk
to knit	on-demand textile fabrication
knit fabric	breathable flexo-tech clothing
yarn	bundled filament
wool	thermo-wicking filament
cotton	high-carbon filament
yarn shop	filament dealer
kettle-dyed	color micro-brewed
handmade	custom

Knitting Language	Guy Talk
needles	fabrication looping tools
knitting tools	gear
needle case	toolkit
lace weight	ultralight
sport weight	(no translation necessary)
bulky	expedition weight
design	engineer
re-design	tweak
shaping	anatomical configuration
seamless	monocoque

Knitting Language	Guy Talk
smooth	low coefficient of drag
sweater	team jersey
designer	team replica
Norwegian style	elite level
Estonian style	pro-tested
pattern	blueprint
embellish	customize
Stitch-and-Bitch	textile fabrication skunkworks
lace	ventilation mesh

Sample conversation:

You: (in a practiced voice) Have you seen my on-demand textile fabrication toolkit? I was thinking of making a control sample with this upgraded, thermo-wicking filament. I just love this deep diesel color.

Him: Huh? Oh, that's your *tool*kit? What kind of gear is that?

You: (thinking fast) These are my Turbo circular fabrication looping tools.

Him: Is that chromed?

You: Something like that . . . . This slick finish creates a lower coefficient of drag with this high-loft filament.

Him: Wow, how did you get all those loops on there so fast?

You: Oh, I've been in training. My coach thinks I'm getting ready to enter the elite level.

Him: (impressed) It looks like you put a lot of sweat into that, but that filament stuff isn't all the same color. And look, some is too thick.

You: The high-end, micro-brewed filament has a lot of variation, but it will make this ventilation mesh design look ultra cool.

Him: Oh, that's a *ventilation system*. Hmm, I thought you were just knitting . . . .

A Favorite Cardigan for Men

If only knitting for the man in your life were this easy.

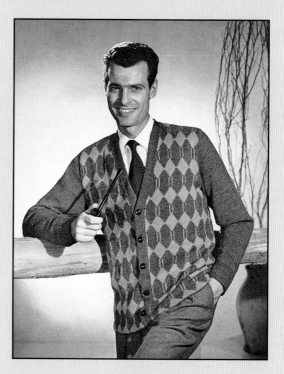